PIANO PIECES & PUZZLES

Level Two

Music and Lyrics by Al Rita and Dan Rita
Activities created and illustrated by Jocelyn Rita

Foreword

This unique series will intrigue and motivate your students to better musical accomplishment. Each book combines progressive piano solos with an activity coordinated with every piece. The lyrics express a wholesome outlook toward personal and social experiences, and the environment.

Enhanced educational value is found in many activities which involve music notation and musical terms. Activities are designed to appeal to a range of ages appropriate to the musical level.

It is suggested that the music be learned first, using the activity as an incentive to finish the music.

9781495081163
I0805708

Schaum Publications, Inc.
10235 N. Port Washington Rd. • Mequon, WI 53092
www.schaumpiano.net

13-07
LC-1

Mister Marvel the Magician

Allegretto ♩= 108–120

Words and music by Al Rita

18
you can plain - ly see.
On then goes the lid.
I count one, two, three!
21
Off now comes the lid.
mf
Oh! it's quite a shock.
Out pops a par - rot who can
24
talk.
I'm
f
Mis - ter Mar - vel the Ma -
gi - cian.
27
See me grab a coin from be -
hind your ear. I'm
Mis - ter Mar - vel the Ma -
30
gi - cian.
Watch this vase of flow - ers
dis - ap - pear!

ABRA CADABRA

Mister Marvel the Magician has made some of the letters in the words below disappear. Complete each word by writing the correct letters as notes on the staff. The first word is done for you.

 + oin = coin

h + 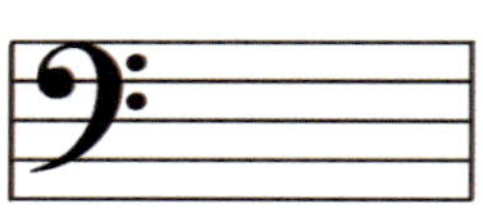 + t = ________

wan +  = ________

ra + 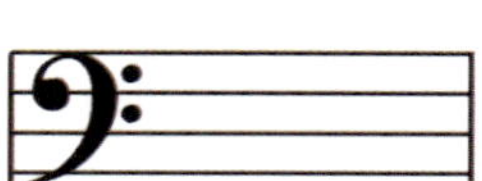 + it = ________

ma +  + ic = ________

p + 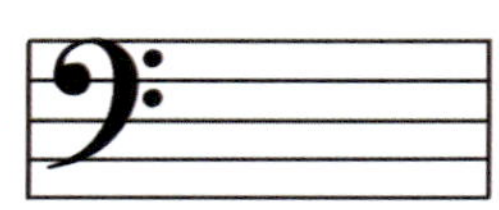 + rrot = ________

 + lowers = ________

m + 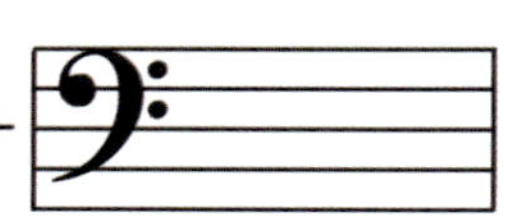 + ician = ________

disapp +  + r = ________

pr + 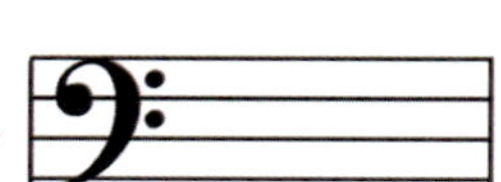 + sto = ________

Timing Is Everything

Fill in the missing time signatures or notes to complete the measures below.

Hint: The measures with no notes may have more than one correct answer.

Time Is

Music by Al Rita
Words by Dan Rita

Cantabile ♩ = 132–152

17
go
tides
turn.
Ev - 'ry - where you
mf
21
go
waves
churn.
f
rit.
mf
25
a tempo
Time
is
ev - 'ry - where
you
go.
mp
29
Time
is
tum - bling
on.
rit.
mf

Meadow Song

Moderato ♩= 112–132

(2nd time play R.H. one octave higher)

Music by Al Rita
Words by Dan Rita

* Morning glories, bluebells and purple trumpets are all different kinds of flowers.

Identifying Intervals

Identify each interval number and its notes below.
The first interval in each line is done for you.

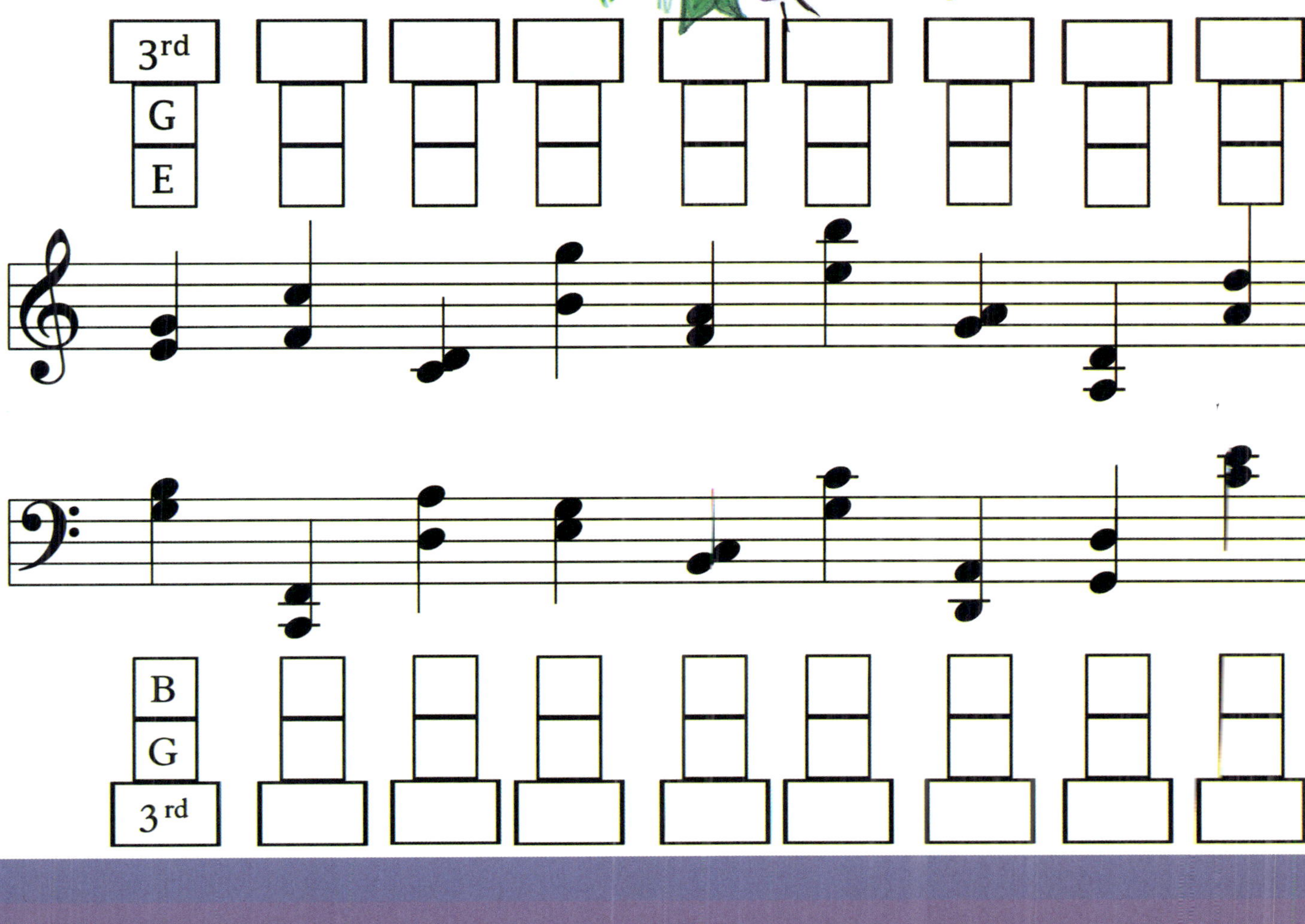

Farm Fair

Music by Al Rita
Words by Dan Rita

Mooooving Notes

Transpose the melody from the key of A Major
to the key of D Major.

When the written work is done, play both lines of music several times at the keyboard.

Birds Are Free, Just Like Me

Music by Al Rita
Words by Dan Rita

Vivo ♩. = 63-70

Birds are free, Just like me.
Wing - ing - ly, swing - ing - ly, spring - ing - ly, sing - ing - ly free.
Hear the wrens and rob - ins chirp - ing,
sing their songs in spring - time's sun - rise. Hear the jays and
star - lings stir - ring, joy - ful in the skies.

Avian Art

Unscramble and draw the squares in their correct places to make a complete picture. The first square is done for you.

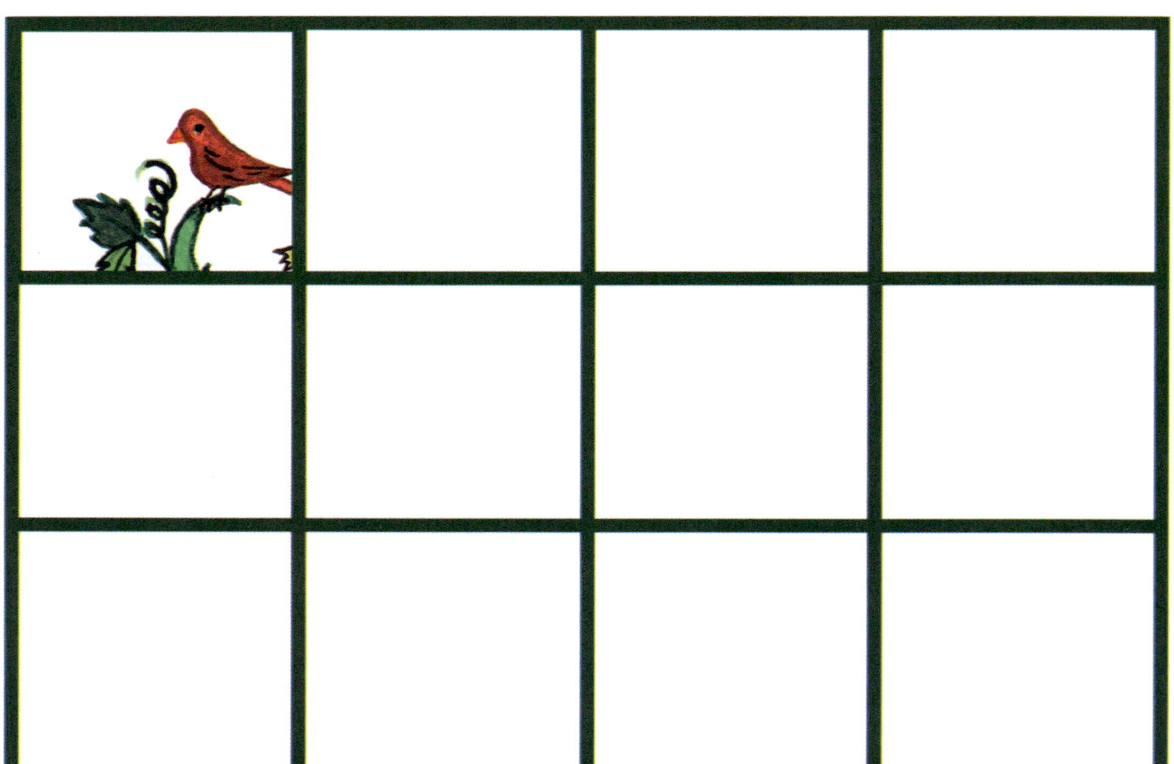

Symbol Sudoku

Complete the puzzle using the different musical symbols below. Make sure that each row, column and 3x3 square contain only one of each symbol. Then fill in the feathers with your favorite colors.

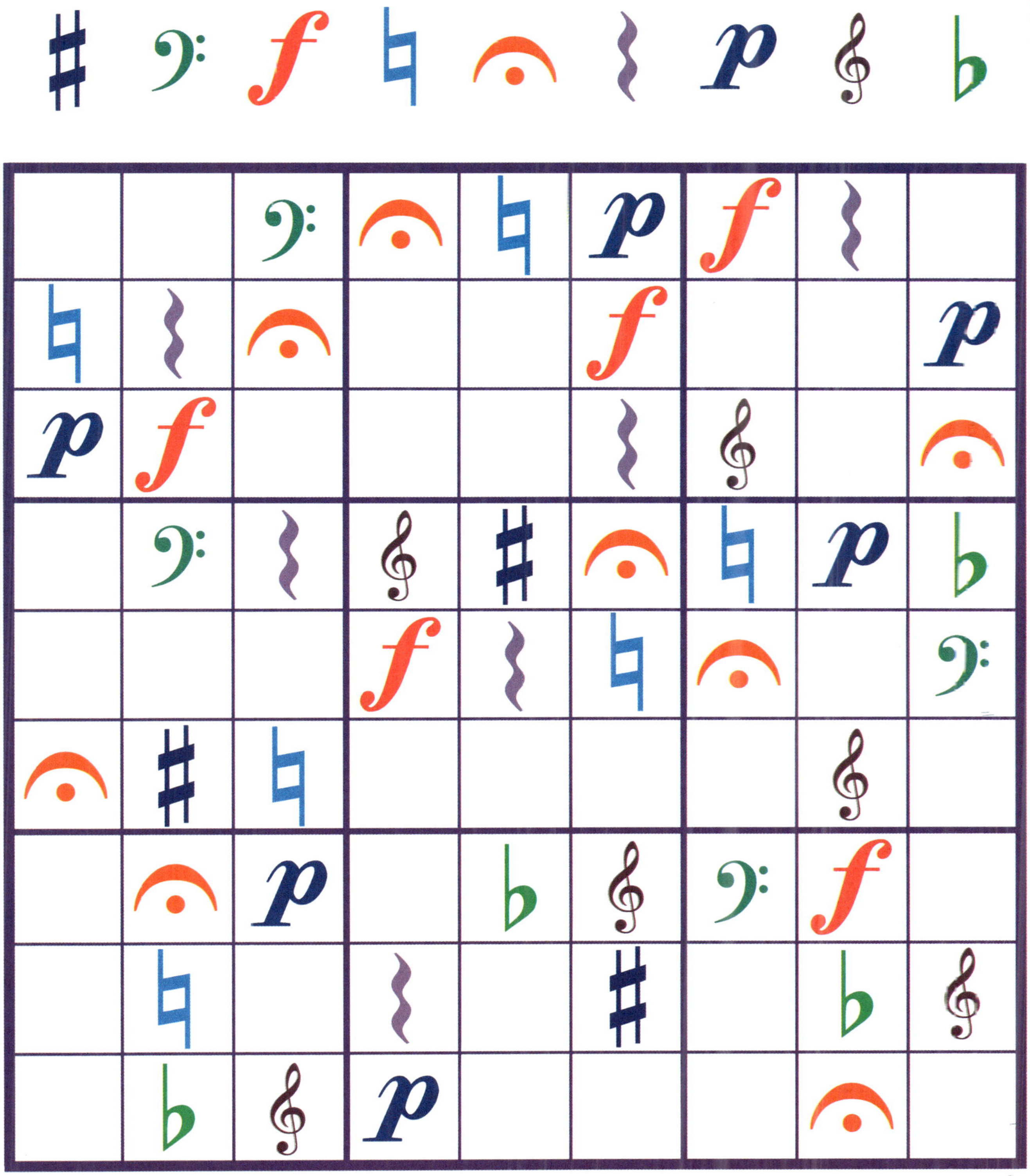

If I Had Wings

Music by Al Rita
Words by Dan Rita

Gently Soaring ♩= 72-80

17
won - der how a bird feels as he sails a - cross the sky.
21
Does he feel light as air when he flies so high? With
mp
rit.
mf
25
feath - er arms, I'd do a - maz - ing things. I'd
a tempo
29
make sky loops, if on - ly I had wings.
f
rit.

Umbrellas in the Rain

Con espressivo ♩ = 108–126

Music by Al Rita
Words by Dan Rita

17
Look at all the col - ors in the um - brel - la crowd! Swirl - ing red and blue and green,
mf
20
Twirl - ing big and bright and loud.
f
23
Um - brel - las in the rain, spin - ning, spin - ning down the street.
mp
27
If the wind blows hard, one might lift you off your feet.
rit.
p
pp

Try a Triad

Write a blocked and a broken triad in ascending (up) or descending (down) order from the note you are given. An example is done for you.

Ex. Descending from the G between Middle C and Treble C

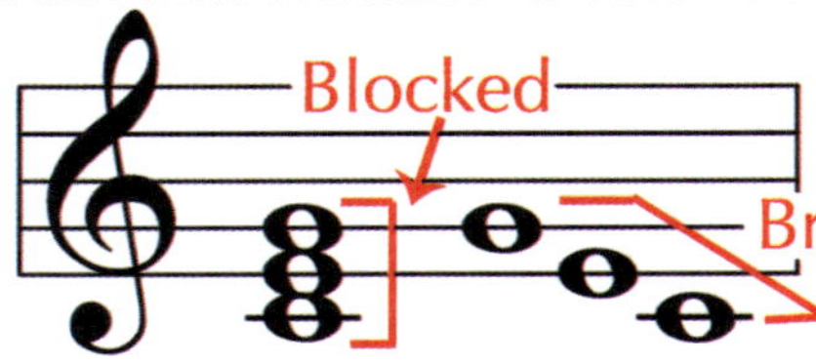

1. Descending from High C

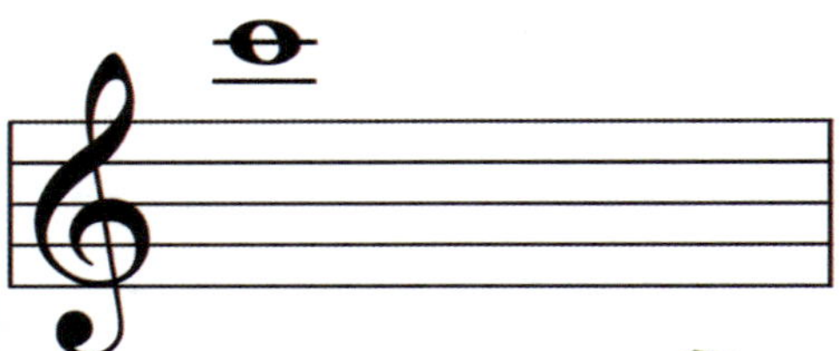

2. Ascending from Bass C

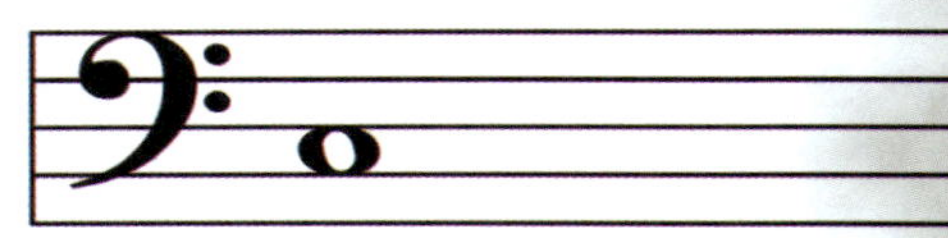

3. Descending from the D above Middle C

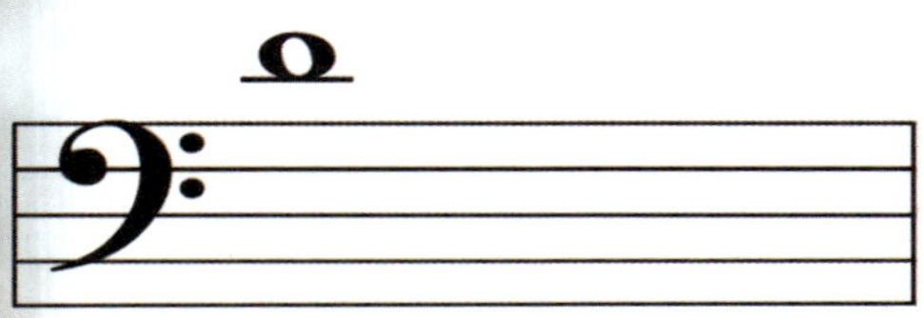

4. Descending from Treble C

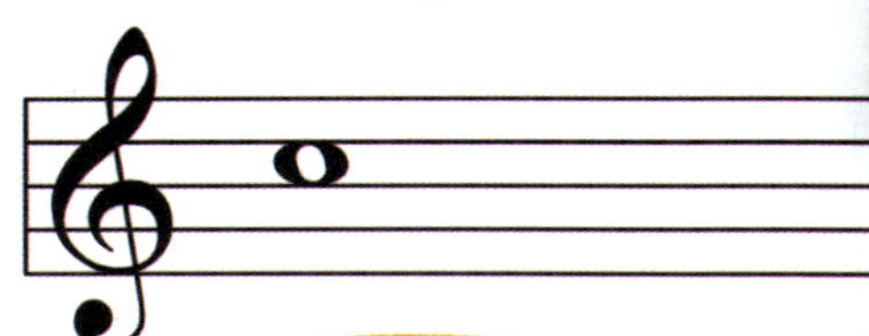

5. Ascending from the D between Treble C and High C

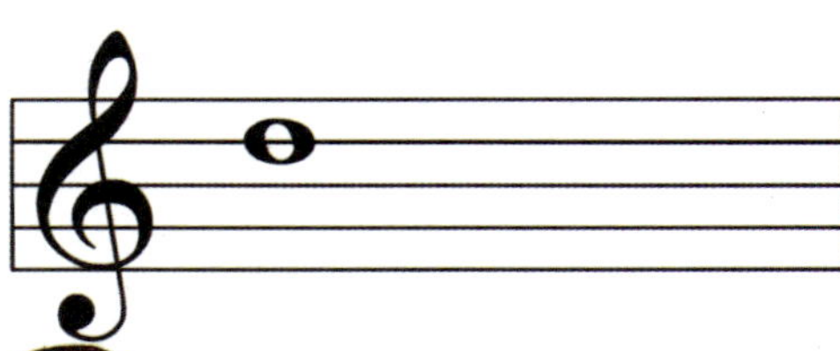

6. Ascending from the F below Bass C

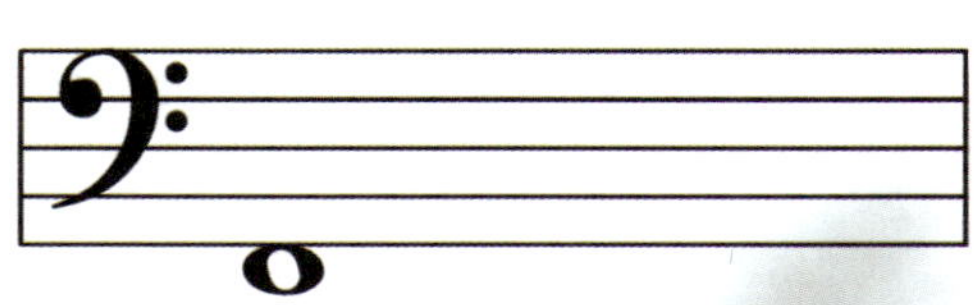

Word Play

Complete the musical crossword puzzle using the clues below.
Use the colorful words around the puzzle if you need help.

ACROSS

1. gradually becoming softer
4. even, flowing
6. playing notes of a chord separately
9. half-tone higher
10. mysterious
13. very lively
14. slow, graceful
15. slow, broad
17. quick, cheerful

DOWN

2. with expression
3. loud
4. light
5. playful
7. gradually becoming louder
8. with spirit
11. detached, short
12. soft
16. half-tone lower

Piano Fun

Words and music by Al Rita

16
Up and down the keys. Le - ga - to, stac - ca - to, two
p
19
touch - es that I know. An - dan - te, Al - le - gro are tem - pos I can go.
22
I will stay sharp and will not fall flat. That's 'cause I prac - tice
mf
25
ev - 'ry day. Play - ing pi - an - o and for - te.
cresc.
28
Up, up, up, and down the keys!
f
rit.
8va

At Our Thanksgiving Day Parade

Words and music by Al Rita

Tur-Key Time

Write the name of each key signature.
The first one is done for you.

G Major

Remember the Golden Rule

Andantino ♩ = 96-108

Music by Al Rita
Words by Dan Rita

Half Stepping

Complete the chromatic passages using the given notes.
An example is completed for you.

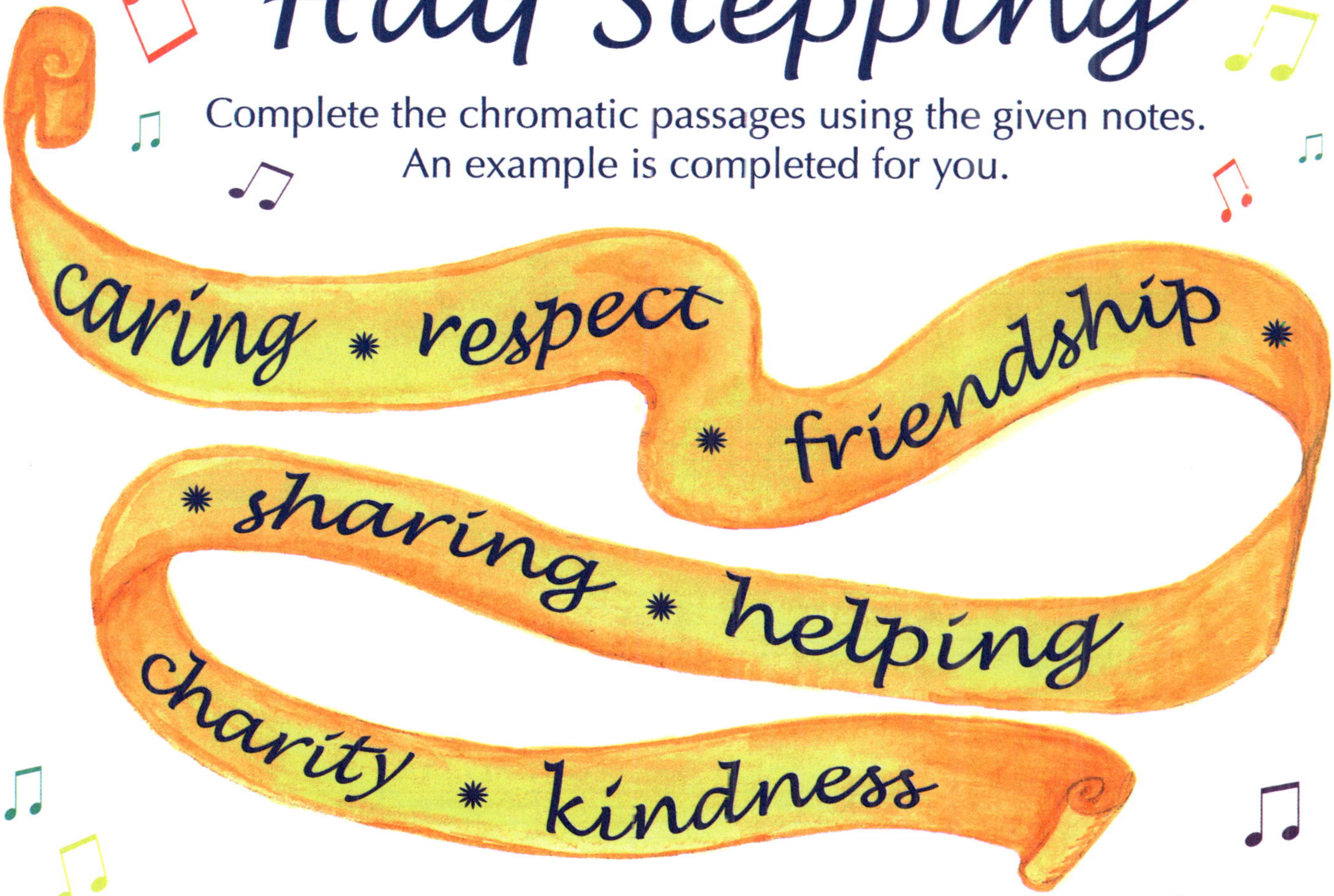

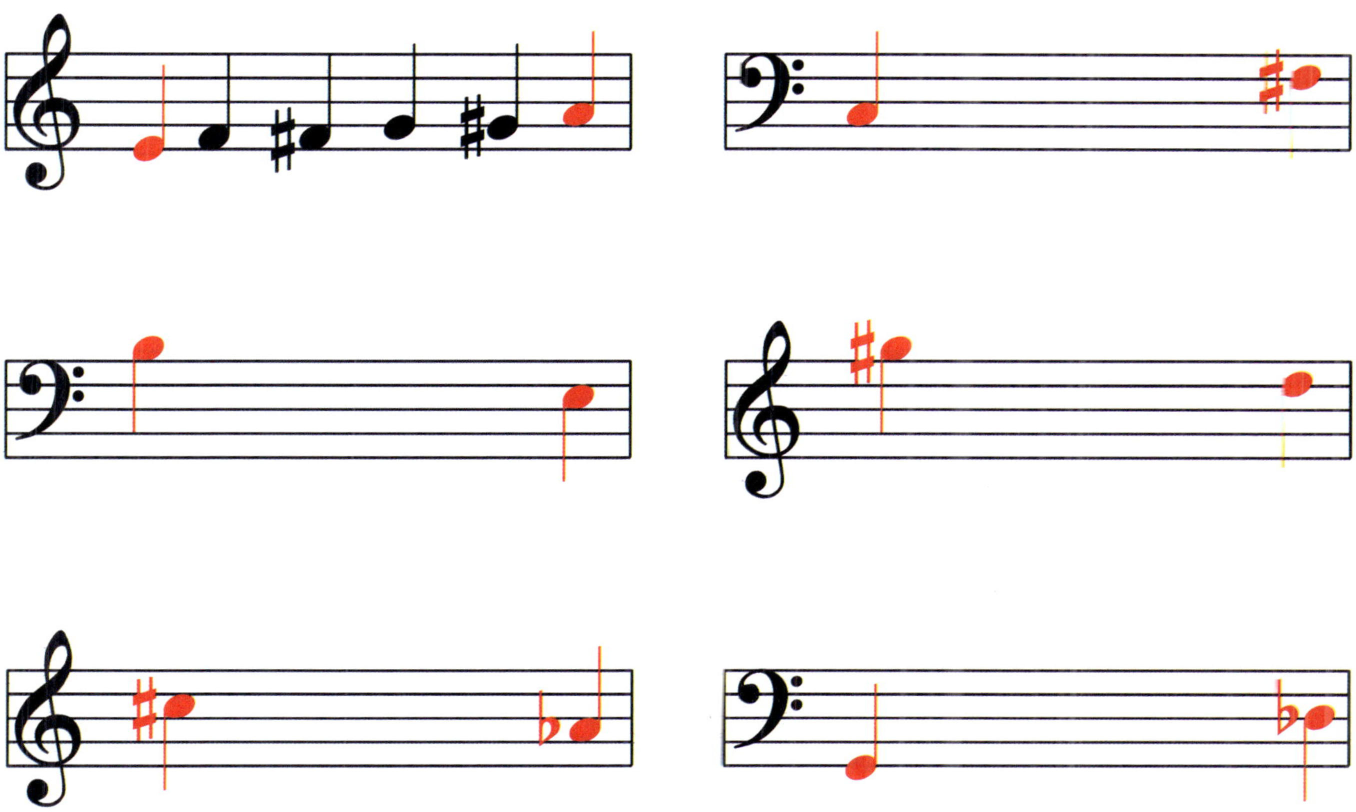

Just a Good Old American Rag

Moderato ♩ = 104–120

Words and music by Al Rita

* The *fandango, Highland fling, tango, swing, jig, polka, shuffle, two-step,* and *reel* are all different kinds of dances.

Music With Moves

Look up, down, forward, backward and diagonally for the dance words below.

I	G	R	B	N	M	C	L	O	G
O	A	A	T	A	P	M	Z	N	N
G	U	B	R	E	T	T	I	J	O
N	J	C	M	R	L	W	S	E	A
A	H	U	U	A	S	L	A	S	T
D	T	M	W	U	S	J	A	W	R
N	B	A	G	Q	A	J	I	B	E
A	G	R	N	S	I	S	A	N	E
F	L	I	N	G	T	T	I	B	L
F	J	A	G	P	O	L	K	A	T

Ballet
Clog
Fandango
Fling
Jig
Jitterbug
Line
March
Polka
Rag
Reel
Rumba
Salsa
Samba
Square
Swing
Tango
Tap
Twist
Waltz

Groundhog Song

Music by Al Rita
Words by Dan Rita

May - be you don't see me, but that's me look - ing out of my
hole. I love my lit - tle home and
so does my best friend, the mole. So
please don't throw the gar - bage and mess up our neigh - bor - hood.
Put it in a trash can. I'd be hap - py if you would.

Clean-Up Crew

Help Groundhog and Mole pick up all the litter and take it to the recycling and trash cans.